More Victorian F

This is my second book
Rossendale', a compilation of local walks published in
1888 by the Rev. James Marshall Mather.

Born in 1851, Mather was a Methodist Minister in
Rawtenstall and Manchester; an acclaimed author
(whose works included two books on John Ruskin);

historian; philosopher and would-be
environmentalist. He wrote as J.
Marshall Mather but was known to
his family and friends simply as
Marshall. Those who knew him said
that he was an inspirational writer
and preacher and combined a
formidable intellect with humility and
empathy with people from all walks of life.

His personality shines through his books and he was,
undoubtedly, an open-minded, compassionate,
engaging and very likeable human being. Shortly after
completing his second 'rambles' book in 1894, he
became seriously ill, possibly with a degenerative
disease, and was unable to walk or speak for the next
twenty years. He died at the age of sixty-five in 1916
and the national magazine of the United Methodists
devoted an issue to his life. He was described as a
genius, interested in everything and everyone, always
seeking truth, yet modest and self-effacing.

1

His style of writing is of its time, delightfully romantic and poetic and he uses far more adjectives than we now deem necessary. His route directions tend to be rather vague and, consequently, one hundred and thirty years later, it can sometimes be difficult to determine exactly where he went but it's very rewarding, using Victorian maps and local knowledge, when the pieces of the jigsaw drop into place.

He rambled at dawn and dusk, alone or with friends and, whatever the weather, time of day or season, he found beauty in his surroundings and sorrow in its despoliation by 'greedy' men.

Since his books were published, housing developments have climbed the valleys' lower slopes but we can still walk on wild moorland, wander through mossy cloughs and admire distant views that Marshall would have known. Did he leave sufficient clues for us to follow his routes today? I decided to find out.

Marshall's Rossendale was different from ours. To us, it is the area currently administered by Rossendale Borough Council, with clear, though arbitrary, boundaries. His was a much less rigidly defined area, known since ancient times as the Forest of Rossendale.

I have selected ten more of Marshall's rambles and reproduced his original text where it relates to the route taken or the social history of the area. I have removed detailed family histories and much of his theological and philosophical commentary. However, some of his musings are so strikingly modern, especially those relating to his and our environment, that I have included them. They provide a surprising insight into the views and concerns of the more-enlightened, deeper-thinkers of his time.

I describe how we can follow in his footsteps. My directions are based on public rights of way that can easily be followed today and, hopefully, will be for decades to come, without the need to read a map or look at a screen.

Chapter headings and text in italics are Marshall's, the remainder are my own.

I hope you find this book interesting and enjoy exploring more of Marshall Mather's Rossendale Valley.

Andrew Gill

Some practical points about walking in Rossendale

It rains a lot here. The moors are often boggy, paths sometimes impassable and the ground underfoot can be very uneven with more trip hazards and slippery slopes than you can wave a stick at and, of course, we have hills .... lots of them. Depending on your level of fitness and ability, you might find the walks in this book physically challenging. Be prepared! Wear appropriate clothing and footwear, make sure someone knows where you're going and, ideally, have a mobile phone with you. Follow the Country Code and please leave my countryside as you find it.

In the more remote areas, especially on the moors, it is easy to lose your bearings and your way and you probably won't meet anyone to ask directions. My routes can be followed without a map and compass but, for your own safety, it is advisable to have them with you and know how to use them.

.... and about following my routes

These routes are for walking, not cycling or driving. I have chosen starting points where you can park nearby or access them by bus or train. Once you start a walk, the footpaths are just that and the lanes are either farm tracks or driveways to private homes, there is nowhere to park or turn-round and the owners are not going to thank you for trying!

Some of the paths and tracks that Marshall used are still public rights of way but are currently difficult to access, as they are obstructed by foliage and fences. Where this is the case, I've chosen better-used alternatives.

I ignore turnings that aren't on the route, so if my directions say go straight on and you find there are paths or lanes to the left or right, feel free to explore them (I can't resist them) but they are not part of the route. I sometimes use clock-face directions: 12

o'clock means straight on; 1 o'clock, bear right; 3 o'clock, turn right etc. All distances are approximate.

There are many stiles and gates on my routes and I don't usually mention them individually, unless I think it will help you find your way.

If you intend to use buses or trains, check timetables as some services are infrequent and others seasonal.

My directions have been independently checked and are, I believe, correct at the date of publication. However, to err is human and if you spot a mistake, please let me know (contact details on the last page). If you find a route that has been obscured, obstructed or diverted, please report it to Lancashire County Council via their website, it's quick and easy to do and they can take appropriate steps to rectify the problem. By doing so, together we will ensure that our rights of way are protected for future generations.

.... and my definitions

Footpath - footpath; **Track** - wider than a footpath, can be vehicle-width; **Lane** - wider and with a better surface than a track; **Clough** - small valley, usually containing a stream; **Gulley** - shallow, valley-shaped depression which might or might not have a stream in it; **Lodge** - a large pond originally used to store water for a mill.

Finally, the disclaimer: you follow my routes at your own risk.

Index of walks

My first book 'Victorian Rossendale Walks' included ten walks, so this one starts with number 11.

Kiln Field Hall

Marshall says: *"There is no part of our district so picturesquely dotted with farmsteads as the Musbury Heights. Slumbering in nooks, or shadowed by plantations, these rude structures of a bygone age yield a delightful relief to the eye of the rambler as he looks down from the summit of the Tor upon the far-reaching, undulating slopes of green. Should he choose to draw nearer to them and stand beneath the shadows of their time-stained gables, his pulse will be sure to quicken as he thinks of their unrecorded annals and mute records of the past. He will remember that within them, for generations, the great drama of life, with its shifting scenes of joy and sadness, has been played and he will discover in their pasturage, traces of the sweat of the forefathers of the hamlet, spilt in the conquest of Nature for the earning of their daily bread.*

Thoughts such as these often possess me as I wander amongst the Musbury farmsteads, and never were they more impressive and suggestive than when, the other day, I stood before the most picturesque and historic of them all, Kiln Field Hall. There is a legend associated with this old hall, the truth of which I cannot vouch for, but which I give as related to me by one who dwells upon the spot. The house is said to have been one of the four "corners," or ecclesiastical boundaries of the ancient parish of Whalley. These "corners" were in the occupation of monks, and during the time of Henry VIII, a certain soldier of renown, for some act of zealous extermination, during the reformation of this reign, was awarded by the King with this estate, which, as far as I can discover, still remains in the hands of his descendants. The building itself carries us back unmistakably some three to four hundred years.

This old house stands beneath the shelter of the quarried heights, and looks down upon the village of Helmshore, some mile distant from its foot.

It is surrounded by a fine plantation of tall trees, wherein the crows have formed a colony. On the south side of the house is a barn, separated from the main block by a well-paved, clean-swept yard, a yard which is a model of neatness and cleanliness. Standing in this yard you face the front of the low-browed house with its well-set walls and gables, and snug, over-hanging roof. The porched entrance is flanked by two thick stone seats, at the end of which hangs the original oaken door, thickly studded with its iron heads. Unfortunately the windows have been replaced, and the dignity of the old structure thereby destroyed; indeed, in archaeological value, it is irreparably damaged.

I was kindly introduced to its interior by the present occupant; but there, too, modern improvement seemed to have shorn it of its original glory. In the kitchen stands a sturdy oaken chest and desk, rudely carved with a device in which the thistle plays a prominent part and bearing the date 1726. This, I ought to say, is not a fixture, but the property of the present occupiers, the good lady showing it to me with no small degree of pleasure and pride. To store our linen in the chest over which our grand-dames stooped, or write our letters on the hard oak boards at which our grandsires sat; to stir our evening cups with the worn and dinted silver once pressed by fingers long since cold, or lie down and sleep upon the stout four-poster whereon some sainted ancestor breathed his last and gave his soul to God, to do these implies the possession of a wealth which a Vanderbilt might well covet, and the princely fortune of a generation's growth strive in vain to purchase.

Passing through the farmyard I followed the flagged path across the meadows towards the heights. The air was clear, and the landscape impressive. I paused to take in the scene that rolled itself out before my eyes, so that it might photograph itself upon the tablets of my mind. It is well to dwell upon the sights that impress us. If we give them time, and permit them to play upon our imagination, they will never leave us, but start forth again and again at our bidding, to gladden us with a never-wearying freshness. I have so endeavoured to approach Nature that my mind now resembles a portfolio, in which are stored many pictures bright and beautiful, and many a recollection of joy and rapture do they bring back as I call them forth to review at will.

As I looked upon this scene I wondered how many inhabitants of Rossendale had witnessed it, and how few there would be who, if they were brought here blindfolded and then relieved of their bandage, could say precisely where they were. I returned by Hill End, dropping down the fields to the reservoir below, and following the Grane Road towards Haslingden.

The sun was now throwing his farewell glory over the heavens. Loneliness was congenial to me, for I wanted to muse upon that which I had seen, so I turned from the wayside to the fields, and slowly paced the Musbury meadows, feeling that the world was "left to darkness and to me," and thus along "the cool sequestered vale I homeward held the noiseless tenor of my way."

Can we follow his route? Yes. This walk explores the slopes of Musbury Heights above Helmshore. To ascend to the 'Heights', see Walk 10 in 'Victorian Rossendale Walks'.

Walk 11: Circular walk from Helmshore Textile Museum to the slopes of Musbury Heights

Distance: 2 miles

Features: a fascinating textile museum; woodland; a disused railway track and lovely views.

Terrain: some not-too-steep gradients; stiles and gates; some very uneven ground; sometimes very muddy in places.

Starting point: Helmshore Textile Museum. Near-ish postcode BB4 4NP.

Parking / Public transport: park at the Museum or on-street nearby. A bus service passes the Museum.

Route: From the Helmshore Textile Museum car park, turn left onto Holcombe Road (B6235) and, in 200 yards, turn right into Park Road. After 50 yards, it bends sharply to the right and becomes a rough track. Continue up the hill and where it widens out (and there is a barn on your left), take the farm lane to the left in the 10 o'clock direction.

Pass through Kilnfield Farm (signed) and take the path up the hill keeping a wall to your left. When a track appears on your right, stay close to the wall on your left. After crossing a stile, turn right onto a track.

Just after it bends to the left, go through the metal pedestrian gate on the embankment to your right. Walk down the footpath, with a wall on your right and emerge next to a house. Keep it on your right then pass another house also on your right. Descend through a field, keeping a wall on your left, then the lane takes a sharp left and a gentle right to a full width gate with a stile to its right. Pass over the stile and turn right.

Where the lane turns sharp left over the reservoir dam, go straight on, up the hill and over the V-pattern stile onto a grass track. Follow it over the wooden boards and descend through a wood to Holcombe Road. At the road, turn right.

At the end of a low wall on your left, go down the steep, stone steps and cross the bridge over Ogden Brook.

Turn right and, in a few yards, at the clearing, bear left to join the surfaced path and turn right onto it. Cross the brook via the bridge and take the left fork.

This is the track-bed of the former Stubbins to Accrington railway line. Continue and it becomes wide, surfaced and walled on both sides (a former viaduct). Just after houses start on your left, where the path divides, take the steps down to the right. At the bottom, turn sharp right through a gate onto a footpath which takes you back to your starting point, the Museum car park.

Deep Clough

Marshall says: *"But few can travel through our valley without admiring the great range of hills that stretch in billowy wildernesses away from Peel's Monument and lose themselves behind the Musbury Tor. Their moorland heights and meadowy lowlands, separated by a line of road, afford rich contrast of colour and of scene, the one being bleak, bare, and brown; the other a wealth of pasturage and wood, of nestling farmstead and outlying fold.*

On their farther side ran the famous Roman road, along which marched the imperial troops; and over their summits devout companies of weary pilgrims wended their way to worship at the Whalley shrine. Over these slopes the huntsmen coursed the deer;

while the rents and dues of their scant pasturage were paid to supply the needs of religious orders or gathered by the exacting and iron hand of manorial lord. Rich in incident is this Holcombe Range; yet little do those who daily travel beneath its shadow, or people its habitations, know of the thrilling incident and old-world association with which its history is fraught.

But Holcome Range is not only rich in history; it is also rich in scenery. The lower slopes are one series of deep-worn cloughs, cloughs overarched with foliage, and ploughed by foaming mountain streams. No less than seven such rend the slopes between the Irwell Vale and Ramsbottom. Ravenshore, Kiln and Kenyon Cloughs are first in order, followed by Deep, Buckden, Ox Hey, and Dick Field. Not one of these but claims a visit: not one of these if visited once but will be visited oft.

They possess a peculiar charm. Wild birds seek their haunt and the startled game rise from their lair; their wealth of wildflower, irradiated by the shaft of sunshine streaming in through opening branches; their many strata, leading back a million years, and telling of rolling seas and settling lakes, vast upheavals, and centuries of accumulation, all these constitute a charm peculiar to these cloughs and make them a favourite haunt of the meditative and imaginative mind.

Deep Clough, sometimes called Hodge Clough, is by far the most picturesque of those dividing the

Holcombe range. To reach it, we take train to Ewood, and, crossing the bridge, turn down by the Co-operative Store and past the Ewood Hall, entering the meadows by the iron gate at the end of the avenue of trees. Here we find ourselves in rich pasturelands. To our right, lies Ewood Out Barn; while a little beyond, and crowning the knoll, stands the quaint old farmstead of Lower Cockham. Below this is Ravenshore Wood, down which the Ogden pours its brawling waters towards Irwell Vale, and where the meadow path we tread now leads.

A distance of half a mile brings us to the bridge that spans this stream; and by following the road between the rows of cottages we pass towards the river banks, and come out at the bridge at Lumb. Here we turn under the viaduct, and pursue our way until we reach the gate that leads to Mr. Holker's house, not neglecting to notice Lumb Hall, originally the seat of Adam Rawsthorne, who lived here in the reign of Edward IV. Beneath the shadow of the railroad and within a stone's throw of the noted paperworks, it stands a relic of old-world life, witnessing to a calmer if not to a more prosperous past.

Passing through the gate, and crossing the field below Mr. Holker's house, we make towards the old vat-shed, and following a footpath that starts from its higher side, we enter Lumb Wood. Below, at a depth of seventy feet, the river winds amid the rocks and falls and bends of this secluded shrine; and but for the manufactory, half hidden by trees and precipice, there would be no break to destroy the perfect serenity and glory of the scene.

From the wood we drop down into the clough, and instead of climbing the further side, we turn towards the right and follow its upward course. Here a little care is called for, else our feet will sink in bog; therefore we shun the shelf of grass that invites us and take the further side of the stream. Once between the gorge, the way is easier, and we soon get a glimpse of its grandeur, and feel that it was rightly named "deep."

The sloping banks suddenly converge and bare their strata, until we find ourselves between well-nigh perpendicular walls of shale and rock. Towards the head of the clough rise two mighty crags of rock, two stony jaws that, opening midway, pour forth in seasons of rain "a slumberous sheet of foam;" in drought, "slow-dropping veils of thinnest lawn." Here we are face to face with Nature in her loneliness and loveliness.

Returning, we walk through the woods towards the Holcombe Road to the adjoining clough of Buckden, which, while not so grand, is none the less as beautiful as the one through which we have passed. The traveller must follow the Holcombe Road, turning off towards Buckden Higher Barn, and thence, passing the house to his left hand, follow the field-path to the foot bridge that spans the higher end of the clough. Many hours have I wiled away in these retreats, where the God of Nature shows His handiwork and breathes the spirit of peace."

Can we follow his route? Yes, most of it. Marshall climbed up the stream-bed of the clough but we will visit the point where he started his ascent and then skirt around the top of it. We will then descend through Buckden Wood and return via the track-bed of the Stubbins to Helmshore railway line and along the banks of the River Irwell.

Walk 12: Circular walk from Ewood Bridge to Deep Clough and Buckden Wood

Distance: 5 miles

Features: a hidden clough, National Trust woodland, waterfalls, disused railway track and riverside walk.

Terrain: some not-too-steep gradients; stiles and gates; some very uneven ground; sometimes very muddy.

Starting point: The junction of Bridge Street, Irwell Vale Road and Blackburn Road (B6527), Ewood Bridge. Near-ish postcode BB4 6LQ.

Parking / Public transport: Park on-street nearby. The Irwell Vale East Lancs Railway Station is half a mile away.

Route: From the road junction walk along Irwell Vale Road for half a mile to Irwell Vale village. Cross the road bridge and go straight ahead into Bowker Street. At the Church, bear right, keeping the Church wall on your left, to a gate and footpath. Walk along the footpath, joining the river on your left, until you reach a road. (The photograph on the back cover was taken from the bridge on your left.) Turn right and pass under the railway viaduct arch into the hamlet of Lumb. Pass Lumb Grange and Old Hall on your left. At the Y junction, bear right up the hill, then after just 20 yards, take the track to the left with the back of the row of houses on your left. We will return to this point after we have visited Deep Clough.

Continue along the track, through a gate, and just before the next gate, take the footpath at

1 o'clock to the right. Continue on this path, with a fence on the left, over a stile, to a tree and marker post where the path divides. Go left down the hill and after a sharp right-hand bend, you'll see a footbridge and a ladder on the far bank.

This is Deep Clough, where Marshall started his ascent. Turn round and retrace your steps to Lumb. At the end of the long row of houses on your right, where the lane bends to the right, go over a stile on your left.

Go up the log steps and climb the hill, keeping a fence on your left. Pass to the right of the new-ish wooden building and continue up the hill with a fence on your right. Cross a wall via a stile and keep going in the same direction. Notice the view of the railway viaduct behind you.

Walk across the field to the farmhouse at 11 o'clock in front of you. Keeping the farmhouse on your right and a solitary tree on your left, walk up the field and pass the farmhouse, to a track on the other side of a wall. Turn left onto the track.

The track bends to the left and slopes downwards towards a wood. Walk to the right of and parallel to a shallow gulley. The top of Deep Clough is in the trees to your left.

Follow the track round to the right and then left, in an arc, over a stream. Within a few yards it begins to bend to the right and, where the track becomes a footpath, turn right up the hill (no path), aiming for the tops of two trees. Continue up the field, midway between the solitary trees on your left and the fence on your right, until you join the main road through a kissing gate. Turn left onto the road (Helmshore Road B6214).

Walk up the road for just under half a mile to a wooded area. Continue along the road until you reach the end of the wood, then cross the stile on the left into Buckden Wood (National Trust, signed). Descend through the wood for half a mile to a metal gate (with a footbridge in front of you). Bear left, at 10 o'clock, and descend, keeping a stream on your right. At the bottom of the hill, at the house on your right, follow the path to the right, around the house, and go through the gap in the wall on the left, onto National Cycle Route 6 and turn left.

This is an old railway line. The East Lancs Railway runs parallel to it on the right, so you might be lucky enough to see a steam train.

Stay on the track for just over half a mile and where it divides (50 yards before a viaduct) bear right down the hill on a winding, surfaced track. At the pedestrian tunnel under the railway on your right, go straight on, keeping the river on your left, to join a road.

Go straight on, with houses on your right and the river on your left until you reach a mini-roundabout. (You can turn right here to visit Irwell Vale Railway Station).

Go straight across the mini-roundabout and turn right onto a narrow path to the right of a farm gate and next to the bungalow garden. After 20 yards, turn left onto the Irwell Valley Way (signed). After a straight section, go under the railway bridge and continue for a quarter of a mile keeping the river on your left. The path climbs away from the river and, at a wooden gate on your left, bear left through it and descend via steps to re-join the river on your left. Pass under a railway bridge and keep the river on your left until you reach a substantial stone bridge with steps from the path up to a road.

Just before the bridge, there is a fine view of Ewood Hall across the river to your left and the area on your right was the location of Ewood Bridge Railway Station where Marshall started and ended his ramble.

Climb the steps, turn left onto the road (Blackburn Road, B6527) and return to your starting point.

Newchurch

Marshall says: *"There is a picturesqueness about Newchurch, especially when seen from Tunstead Lane and Piper Cote. The bold brow of the site gives to the village a striking prominence and this is still further thrown out by the sweeps of Cowpe and heights of Seat Naze on either hand. The quaint dwelling-houses, as they rise, tier above tier, with their irregular gables and steep pitched roofs of slab and slate, are grouped into a unity and overshadowed with a dignity by the massive, grey, square turreted tower of the kirk, while patches of green, and the wooded demesne of mansions, add beauty and restfulness to the scene.*

To stand at Piper Cote at the hour of sunset and look across the intercepting valley to this little knoll of habitation on the farther side is to look upon one of the most picturesque sights that Rossendale can boast.

Let us climb by Thistle Mount and turn up Old Street, once the High Street of the little town, but now supplanted by a road less steep, and better suited to our modern methods of domesticity and travel. As we ascend, we find ourselves overshadowed by houses of an ancient date, and our thoughts go back to days of old. We think of the hardy race once peopling them, men and women to whom the shriek of whistle and the roar of manufacture were unknown; whose little world was their valley, and whose farthest journey was the summit of some neighbouring hill. We climb the steep, and halt before a row of dilapidated dwellings, with mullioned windows and Tudor-arched doors, now one of the oldest inhabitable blocks in the valley.

At present the homes of poverty, they were once peopled by the rich. Beneath their crumbling roofs, the twin mysteries of birth and death fulfilled the mission of joy and sorrow. Over their well-worn thresholds, youthful hope has stepped with wild enthusiasm to face a world; and sorrow, with its sin-sown tears, returned to lay its burden down at home.

Now we face the good old hostel bearing the date 1674. Who can recall the illustrious great who in their day halted and rested here? Who can recount "the quips and cranks and wanton wiles" cracked over the white-topped tables, when foaming nut-brown ale was served in shining pewter? Who can re-tell the arguments, political and social, fought out in wordy warfare, or the tales told over the winter's fire?

Continuing our way, we pass a house of more pretentious build, and once the vicarage, standing in shadow behind its iron palisades and fronted by plots of mildewed grass. It wears an eerie look, and should we approach it as the neighbouring clock strikes out the midnight hour, rumour tells us we should hear the trailings of ghostly garments and behold the spectres of the past.

Passing along the street towards Rawtenstall, other buildings of an old-fashioned structure arrest the eye; not least among them being the shop over whose portal are inscribed the words "Within this shop we can afford; Goods fresh and cheap, upon my word." This inscription cannot be read without a thought as to how the merchandise of those days would match the adulteration which competition now compels even the honest tradesman to dispense with his food supplies.

The original village of Newchurch was Booth Fold, which to this day is spoken of as "the ancient city." Here the first families grouped and housed themselves, two brothers of the name of Ashworth dating back to the year 1297. The original church, a wooden structure and built in the year 1510 or 1511, and the product of the spontaneous labour of the country folk, stood a little below the present building in what is still known as Chapel Croft. For fifty years it met the needs of a scanty and impoverished people, after which it was rebuilt upon the present site in a more substantial form.

The second church, built in 1561, was altered, enlarged, and remodelled from time to time to meet the needs of an increasing population; but in 1824 it was taken down and rebuilt. There is nothing whatever attractive about the architectural features of the present church. The peal of bells is its one redeeming feature. These sweet-toned ministrants may be heard, all too seldom, beating out their music upon the evening air, the wind wafting their melody in waves of liquid song across the moorland sweeps and along the valleys to the village home.

There are inhabitants still living whose parents were wont to tell of a fall of snow which blocked up Old Street to the height of eight or ten feet, and necessitated the sleighing of coffins containing corpses for interment upon the frozen surface to the then entrance gates of the churchyard.

Newchurch is rich in local interest. For generations it was the centre of the feasts and holy days and famed for mirth and jollity. The mummer and morris dancer played to its crowds and tripped along its narrow streets; and to this day its fair is by far the most famed in the neighbourhood. The bull was baited in Booth Fold, the ring to which the brute was secured having lately been removed and there was an important annual race meeting on Seat Naze.

It is said that Englishmen take their pleasures sadly. This was not always so and though we do not wish to go back to the rude forms of mirth adopted by our ancestors, we nevertheless commend the reality and naturalness which characterised them, and which are so sadly wanting in many of the forms of modern pleasure. Modern enjoyments are sought outside natural methods and domestic limits and therein lies their curse. Distance is deemed a requisite and expense an essential. Not so in the hey-day of old Newchurch life. Granted the world was narrow and the frolic local; yet these conditions made it all the more real and delightful. Thus, while shrinking from its brutality, we commend its homeliness and inexpense.

At one time the crucible and the mint were to be found in the sheltered nooks of Newchurch, a gang of forgers and coiners surreptitiously issuing counterfeit coin of the realm. The village also supplied a contingent to the great Chatterton fight but after flying at the sight of red, they wandered in terror upon the moors, visited the neighbouring towns in disguise, and at last returned to their native village, crestfallen, and vowed they would "never do so no more."

One of the most interesting features in Newchurch is the adoption and common use of bye-names. The old burial records kept by the early sextons afford a most amusing study. We find entries such as: "James o' Edmund's o' Thomas's," "George' lad o' great Jim's," "John Lord o' Little Dick's," "Oliver o' deaf Martha's," "Jovil," "Poor Tike," "Owd Loll," "Rough 'ead," "Iron ears." The study of these names is of the greatest interest, for it takes us back to the time when the character and the ancestry of the man were more important factors in naming him than the baptismal font. Though education is doing much to wear away these customs, many of them still remain. Not many years ago a doctor in Rossendale, while examining a boy prior to granting a certificate for half-time employment in the mill, asked of him his name. "Tom o' Sam's," said the lad. "But what's your Father's name?" again queried the man of science. "Sam o' Deborah's," was the simple reply. "Then what's your mother's name?" roared out the perplexed practitioner. "Moll o' Nan's," answered the lad in all sincerity. The doctor looked hard at the boy for a moment and seeing that what had been said had been said in good faith, turned upon his heel, exclaiming: "Well! you come of a devil of a breed and no mistake."

There is an air of quiet reigning round this ancient hamlet. No mills mar its streets and its larger dwellings are freed from the modernism that spots the architecture of nineteenth century wealth and pride. To those whose joy in the present is to people the past, to whom the times of old teem with an ever absorbing life, and to whom a historic church possesses a peculiar charm, a turn through the winding walks and a glimpse at the irregular dwellings of this ecclesiastical centre of Rossendale is a profitable and pleasurable diversion amid the din and dirt of this all absorbing commercial valley."

Can we follow his route? Yes. Marshall's initial vantage point was a farmhouse, Piper Cote, which we will pass. However, because of new buildings and tree growth, we have to climb further up the hill behind it, on Tunstead Lane, to get a similar view to his and, even then, it's a rather restricted one. From there, we descend into the village, using some footpaths that he would have been familiar with.

Walk 13: Circular walk around Newchurch

Distance: 2 miles

Features: parks, woodlands and an interesting Churchyard.

Terrain: some fairly steep gradients; uneven ground; some parts can be muddy, especially in Booth Fold Wood.

Starting point: The entrance to Trickett's Memorial Ground, Burnley Road East. Near-ish postcode BB4 9AU.

Parking / Public transport: Park on-street nearby. Bus services pass the Memorial Ground entrance.

Route: From the Trickett's Memorial Ground arch, walk up Burnley Road East and turn right onto Booth Road. Cross the river bridge and turn left into Todd Carr Road. At the end, at the road junction, turn sharp right up a narrow, straight footpath with a metal hand-rail. Continue for 150 yards to Park Road, then turn left. The road bends to the right, stay on it, keeping the park on your left until you reach a T junction, Edgeside Lane. Turn right.

In 200 yards, just before the school building on the right and immediately after the last house on the left, (which was, in Marshall's day, Piper Cote), take the footpath up the hill to the left in the 10 o'clock direction. This is Tunstead Lane. Continue for 250 yards, keeping the wood on your right until you reach two, small, metal gate-posts. Turn round to see Marshall's view of Newchurch. Retrace your steps to Edgeside Lane and turn right.

Pass Park Road and the children's play area on your left and turn left through the gates of Edgeside Park. Descend on a wide path to a path T junction and turn right. Pass a play-area and, at a path T junction, turn right, exiting the park at a road junction.

Turn left, then immediately right in a 2 o'clock direction onto Wales Road with a wall, then the backs of terraced houses, on your left. The road soon bends to the right and the wooded valley on your left is Booth Fold.

You now have a choice. You can descend through the wood or stay on Wales Road and skirt around it. To go through the wood, 30 yards after the end of the terraced houses, go through the gap in the wall on your left and follow the path, which bears right and goes down steps to a clearing. To skirt around the wood, stay on Wales Road and after a left bend and just before the bridge over the river, turn left onto a wide track and follow it until you can go no further. Either option brings you to a footbridge over the river.

Cross the bridge, turn left onto Burnley Road East and then right into Hippings Lane. Take the footpath on the left, into the trees with a stone-slab fence on its left side.

At the top, cross the road (Turnpike) onto Old Street, then walk up the street to the short, cobbled section at the top.

Turn left at the road junction onto Church Lane with the Church and churchyard on your left. If the gates are open, I recommend spending some time in the churchyard looking at the gravestones.

Where the road bends to the right, take the walled path on the left in the 11 o'clock direction. After 100 yards, opposite a gap in the right-hand wall, turn left onto a footpath towards the trees. Where it divides, take the right fork and descend into the wood. The path widens out and then bends to the left. Continue until you reach your starting point, Trickett's Memorial Ground (Marshall's 'Thistle Mount') gates.

The Dawn from Cribden

Marshall says: *"I do not wish my readers to suppose from this title that I am about to sing the praises of early rising. I could consistently do so, but as the Rambler does not set himself up to be a preacher, philosopher, or moralist, it would be out of place to attempt it. There is a greater mystery in the dawn than in the twilight, and a greater solemnity too, for then the day's deeds are possibilities, while at night they have become actual facts, what is written is written indeed.*

Monday morning last saw me an early riser. Before the whistles warned of the approaching hour of six, I was making preparation for a ramble. As I stepped out into the open air, Nature wrapped me around and fanned my face with what to me are her most refreshing airs, airs blowing from the north-west. I love that north-west wind. Is it not prophetic of a clear horizon and a glorious day?

Leisurely walking along the Haslingden Road I took a turn and here lingered to listen to a solitary robin perched upon the topmost bough of an age-worn alder. When I gained the brow of the Old Road, I paused to take a survey of the hills around me. There, before me, were the mountains, topped with glory and engulfed in gloom, their extreme slopes hidden in the haze of dawn. A moment more and the landscape altered with a suddenness almost surprising as, once over the brow, the Burnley and Bacup valleys disappear and the Ramsbottom and Grane valleys start into sudden prominence. What a difference on this, the morning of my ramble, between the towns of Rawtenstall and Haslingden. Rawtenstall was cloud-capped whereas Haslingden was lit up by the beams of the rising sun and swept of its night exhalations and mists.

I now passed up by "Spout House" so called from the flush of waters bursting forth from the hill at its rear. Should the rambler follow them he will find they pass through the lower fields to Lonsdale's Buildings, where they are utilised by Messrs. Ormerod's for sizing. Thence they flow onward to the foundries, and to the reservoirs of Syke-Side. Next, the woollen works of Messrs. Smith are served by their volume, to be afterwards delivered at the Fall River Weaving Shed. From this point they flow towards the Holme, emptying themselves through the grounds of Joshua Townsend, Esq. into the Irwell below. Few people dream of the mighty work which this spout of water accomplishes in its short and circuitous course.

Spout House played a prominent part in the Sunnyside Print-Work Riots of 1832. There had been a dispute as to the overs of the blocks, and the feeling between masters and men ran so high that violence was threatened. As Mr. Brooks was returning from Haslingden he was discovered and pursued by an infuriated mob, and he sought safety in Spout House. But even in a shelter such as this it was felt that one against such odds ran imminent risk; so it was determined to practise a ruse upon the attacking forces. A child was despatched with a can, on the pretence that she was on her way for milk. In this can, however, was a note from Mr. Brooks to the resident magistrate at Haslingden, for the immediate despatch of the military. They soon arrived and the lady is still living in Rawtenstall who, kneeling in the window bottom of the besieged house, saw the red breasts of the soldiers rise above the brow of the hill below. The rioters soon fled, hotly pursued and madly belaboured. One of the ring-leaders, known as "Old Joan," was so thoroughly exhausted with the chase that when he arrived at the bottom of the hill he fell down in a state of collapse, and had not a quick-witted woman covered him with a bran tub close at hand he would have suffered severely at the hands of his pursuers. Another rioter, feeling the hot breath of a charger upon his shoulders and neck, and knowing that another stride or two meant death, turned suddenly aside, and threw himself into a well, where he remained for some time up to his waist in water. The soldier was afterwards heard to say that in the gathering dusk he imagined the earth had opened and engulfed the man.

From Spout House I climbed the rocky rut towards the old and higher road that leads to Cribden, the road originally used by the pack-horses between Accrington and Haslingden to Crawshaw Booth and Newchurch. I next bent my back to climb the steeps of Cribden. This hill, which rises to a height of 1,317 feet above sea level, was originally called Criddon, or Keirn Don, the hill of stags. The name is indicative of the character and haunts of old Rossendale, as it was upon eminences such as this that stags congregated in hot weather, while the fallow deer grazed upon the slopes below.

An imposing view of the surrounding country is gained from its summit. Should the day be clear the town of Bury may be seen to the south, and in certain lights the sparkle of the sea on the western coast. On this, the morning of my ramble, I was too late for sunrise, and I missed the clear cold light which I anticipated, a light peculiar to the day's earliest hours. Looking down towards Haslingden, my eye rested upon the Laund Hey, the flat of land lying below and once the ground upon which the noted races were run. The old steward, Peter Sale, was well known and he sacrificed a large fortune which he might have inherited from his uncle, Henry Wilkinson, had he only fallen in with the old man's condition, and renounced the turf.

And so the early morning hours sped on until the duties of the day reminded me that I was wanted below. I returned, better in heart and body. True indeed are the words of an old philosopher "When you are thirsty drink water; when you are low-spirited drink oxygen." This long, enjoyable quaff, my pint of morning and of mountain air, filled me with new life, braced me for a day's labour, quickened my relish for food, plain yet good, and stirred those deeps of soul which tend to keep a man grateful, happy, and good tempered towards his fellows."

Can we follow his route? Yes. Marshall was the Minister at the Rawtenstall United Methodist Church which is now St. Mary's Chambers and he lived nearby, so we start from there to follow his early morning walk.

Walk 14: Rawtenstall to the summit of Cribden

Distance: 4.5 miles (there and back)

Features: Spectacular views from the top and a unique landmark on the way.

Terrain: A continuous climb with some steep gradients; some very uneven ground; can be very muddy.

Starting point: St. Mary's Chambers, Rawtenstall. Postcode BB4 6QX

Parking / Public transport: Park on-street nearby. The starting point is close to Rawtenstall Bus Station and East Lancs Railway Station.

Route: Walk along Haslingden Road away from Rawtenstall town centre. Pass 'The Whittaker Museum and Gallery' (well worth a visit) and Mount Street on your right and, at the end of the next row of houses (Cornall's Buildings), turn right onto a narrow footpath (signed). Climb the hill for a quarter of a mile,

cross a road (Haslingden Old Road) and continue up the hill on a track then footpath, keeping a wall on your right, until you reach a lane (Oakenhead Wood Old Road). Turn left onto the lane.

After a third of a mile, the lane gently bends to the right. Soon, where it bends sharply down to the left, go straight on, on a stone footpath. After a further quarter of a mile, just after two adjoined houses on your left, the lane bends to the left at a Y shaped junction. Take the right fork onto a stone track.

This is Spout House Farm, mentioned by Marshall, and the 'spout' is on your right at the

junction. On the day that I photographed it, it spouteth not!

At the top of this track, at the junction with a lane (Cribden End Lane), we are going to turn right towards the communications mast but you might want to visit the 'Halo' first. It is a large modern sculpture, illuminated at night.

To do this, instead of turning right, do a left / right dog leg and bear left through the gate by the information board, into 'Top o' Slate'. The Halo is 200 yards along the path. The views from here are spectacular.

If you are not visiting the Halo, turn right at the track / lane junction onto a walled farm lane. Pass to the left of the communications mast and continue for about half a mile.

At the point where the lane bends to the right, pass through a gap in the wall on your left and turn sharp left.

Follow the path around to the right, keeping a wall on your left and just before the full-width / pedestrian gate, turn sharp right in a 4 o'clock direction, up the hill, so that a wall / fence is on your left. Continue up the hill, keeping the wall / fence on your left until, at the top, you reach a metal kissing gate. Turn left through the gate and continue for 200 yards, keeping a wall on your left. You've now reached the summit of Cribden. I hope you agree that the view was worth the climb.

We will return by the same route, the main points of which are:

- return to the kissing gate, turn right and descend, keeping the wall on your right
- at the bottom of the hill turn left and skirt the hill to the gap in the wall
- turn right, pass the mast and, at the lane junction, turn left onto the stone track
- at the 'spout' bear left onto another track
- at the next junction, where a lane joins from the right, go straight on
- follow the lane to the hamlet and just before the first house on the right, turn right onto a footpath
- descend to Haslingden Old Road and cross it
- descend to Haslingden Road, turn left and return to your starting point, St. Mary's Chambers.

Alden and Hare Cloughs

Marshall says: "*A point of centre is always a help to a rambler; a beacon brow, a heathery knoll, or other special natural features, around which he may hover, and to which he may turn when in uncertainty as to his whereabouts. To me the Tor of Musbury has long possessed features such as these and, when lost on some wild moor, its heathery crown assures me of my bearings.*

On Monday last I felt its drawings and yielded myself up to them. I rapidly made my way to Stake Lane Bar. Here, four roads meet, and here in times gone by, the bodies of criminals were quartered and staked, while in the nursery, a little to the left, the jibbet once stood, where the bleached bones of those suspended rattled in the breeze.

Following the Alden Road I soon found food for observation. On either side of this track, in the hedge-rows and ditch-bottoms, grow the Alder tree and Holly bush. To the right, flanked by the Alden Clough, rose the meadow lands of Musbury, their rich pasturage throwing into striking relief the bare, brown moors on the farther side, with their scantily dotted dwellings and sharp scarped tops; while towering above the gorge were the heights of Alden, stern and gloomy, as in sharp outline they stood out against the sky.

After reaching a block of houses known as Alden Row, I branched off from the road which leads into the quarries and struck up by Wood Side Farm and by keeping to the cart tracks, and, where these cease, to the footpath which diagonally crosses the topmost field, came out at Dover Farm, now uninhabited and fast falling into decay. By the side of this house runs a rough moorland road leading on towards Goose-pits, another uninhabited and dilapidated farmstead. By persistently following this now unused path, and by dint of much bog-trotting and careful treading, I reached the basin, or land-bay of Alden, a mighty sweep, semi-circular in form, bounded on the one hand by Musbury and on the other by the Holcombe Ridge.

Upon reaching this sanctuary of the hills, I paused that I might take in the impressiveness and grandeur of the scene. A silence reigned, broken only by the cry of the teewit and the distant carol of the lark, the far-off voice of a shepherd tending his sheep in the vale below and the drip and ripple of the falling stream. Shut in thus, far from the madding crowd, and away from the world's ignoble strife, I mused upon the littleness of life, and the strength and majesty of the everlasting hills.

Following the winding track I passed the foot of the mountain cataract, where, in years gone by, many came from far that they might stand beneath its waters and be reinvigorated with its shower of spray, for, in those days, I was told by an old inhabitant, it was a common thing for the invalid thus to try the efficacy of this mountain fall, and oftentimes to return acknowledging its cure.

I now drew up towards the well-known house, which together with its limited acreage, forms the farmstead of Pilkington. As I approached, I entered into conversation with a rosy-faced moorland lad, who at first viewed me somewhat suspiciously, but who, on gaining confidence, chatted freely in the dialect of the hills. On the farther side of the house a tablet is reared, bearing inscriptions respectively to "my sisters," "my brothers," and "my mother," and commencing…. "To dwell in harmony and love, was woman's mission ever." Upon inquiry, I found it was the composition of a young man who, in some reckless moment, left home for foreign shores, and who, on coming to himself, wrote these lines and forwarded them to the loved ones left behind, who, in their turn, inscribed them upon this slab as a memorial.

I now kept the flagged path along the hillside, passing Black Isle, and crossing the road lately laid by Mr. Porritt over the tops. These tops are being rapidly brought under cultivation. A word or two with the horny-handed tillers of these moorlands, and a peep into the cribs where oxen lay at the Burnt Hill Farm, and then a drop down to the gate some hundred yards below, brought me, after a rapid descent of the fields, to the wood bridge crossing the Hare Clough stream.

Down this clough I plunged with many a leap and slip, stopping now and again to look around me at the sylvan scene. Towards the outlet the stream widened and soon the ruins of the old mill came in view, and through the dismantled walls the rusted spokes of the waterwheel were seen. Following the stream I came out by Tanpits and hasted towards my home.

And so, after taking six hours for the circuit, I ended my day's ramble amongst the lone mountains and moorland cloughs around the Tor. Of fatigue I felt none, and I was loth to return. The leisurely pace, the soft and yielding sward, the bracing breeze, the ever-varying scene, all these reinvigorated the body and made the ramble as delightful as the day.

It has been said a man's character stands revealed in the aspects of Nature he most loves. For me, mountains and moors possess a spell which no other manifestations of Nature wield; the heather and the cotton grass, the cry of the wild fowl and the plaintive note of the plover bird, the freedom that encircles, the silence that reigns."

Can we follow his route? Alden Clough and Hare Clough are in two valleys separated by Musbury Tor. Marshall started his walk in the Alden Valley and crossed over the moor top to drop down into Hare Clough and thence back to his starting point. We can follow much of his route within each valley but, unlike Marshall, can only cross from one to the other by almost returning to our starting point. I have, therefore split his walk into two, numbers 15 and 16.

Walk 15: Circular walk around the Alden Valley

Distance: 2.5 miles

Features: Quiet, rural paths and lanes; a Victorian hamlet and lovely views.

Terrain: some fairly steep gradients; some uneven ground; can be muddy in places; we cross a stream without a bridge which can be impassable after prolonged rain.

Starting point: The junction of Alden Road, Free Lane and Holcombe Road, Helmshore. Near-ish postcode BB4 4LU. In Marshall's day, this was Stake Lane Bar where, he says, *"the bodies of criminals were quartered and staked, while in the nursery, a little to the left, the jibbet once stood, where the bleached bones of those suspended rattled in the breeze."*

Parking / Public transport: Park on-street nearby. The starting point is about half a mile from a bus route.

Route: Walk along Alden Road, ignoring lanes to the right and left, for half a mile, until you reach a row of cottages on your left. This is Alden Row. Continue along the lane and, at the block of garages, bear right, over a stile, onto a grass track. There is a lodge, then a fence and stream (Alden Brook) on your right.

Cross a stile next to the stream, then cross the stream (no bridge) and turn left on the other side. Follow the path up the hill keeping a fence on your left.

The derelict farmhouse on the hillside to your left, at 10 o'clock, is Dover Farm that Marshall mentions.

When you reach a wall, turn right, up the hill, keeping the wall on your left.

Where the wall ends, turn left, over a stile, so that another wall is now on your right.

At this point, where the photograph above was taken, the remains of Marshall's 'Farmstead of Pilkington' are on the hillside in the 10 o'clock direction but not visible from here. He walked over the moors from there to the next valley (See Walk 16). Continue, keeping the wall on your right, towards the house in front of you. Pass to the right of the house and turn right onto a lane.

Follow the lane for one third of a mile (including a left / right 'S' bend) and, after a stone horse trough on your left, at a farm gate, follow the road to the right, down the hill. Keep the farm buildings on your left and, at a T junction with a wooden electricity pole on the corner, turn right and descend towards the trees. Follow the lane, passing Tor Side Hall on your left, until you reach rows of terraced cottages on your left.

At their mid-point, the road bends to the right. Stay on it as it narrows and climbs towards a wood.

 Continue up the hill with the wood on your left and a field on your right. At the top, bear left onto a lane (Alden Road) and return to your starting point.

Walk 16: Circular walk from Helmshore Textile Museum to Hare Clough and the Musbury Valley

Distance: 4 miles

Features: lovely views in a quiet valley "far from the madding crowd".

Terrain: some fairly steep gradients; uneven ground; some parts can be muddy, really muddy!

Starting point: Helmshore Textile Museum. Near-ish postcode BB4 4NP.

Parking / Public transport: park at the Museum or on-street nearby. A bus service passes the Museum.

Route: From the Helmshore Textile Museum car park, turn left onto Holcombe Road (B6235) and, in 200 yards, turn right into Park Road. In 50 yards, follow it round to the right. In 120 yards, opposite the last house of a row of houses on the right, turn left onto a wide stone track.

Follow this track for a quarter of a mile, then around the end of two cottages and cross a small, concrete bridge over a stream. Take the path to the left of a gate, next to the stream. Cross over a stile, then continue along the track, parallel to the stream which is in a gulley over to your left.

In a third of a mile, after the start of a wood on your right and a gate with a stile, the path divides. Take the right fork keeping the wood on your right. This is Hare Clough and we will stay with it for some time.

A little further on, after another gate, where the track bends to the left, cross the stream to go through the gate on your right, then turn left towards the trees. Cross the stream again, then follow the path as it meanders up the hill, keeping the trees and gulley on your right. Pass through a pedestrian gate, and continue

uphill, parallel to the gulley which is now on your left.

At the stone 'dam' on your left, bear right then immediately left to continue up the hill, still with the gulley on your left.

When your path merges with another, bear left onto it, and soon a wall comes into view on the skyline at 11 o'clock.

The path goes to the left end of the wall and, just 10 yards later, at a stile in the wall, turn left towards the solitary trees.

We are going to stay on this path for the next three miles. Some of it is part of the Rossendale Way and there are several RW signs along the route. We will follow the path along this side of the valley, with Musbury Tor to our left, then around the top end of the valley and finally return on the other side, below the Tor, all at mid-height between the hill tops and the valley bottom. The path is easy to follow but has few landmarks, so the photographs below are some of the sights that you'll pass on the way. The slopes that you can see in the 10 o'clock direction are where Marshall came down from the moors with *"many a leap and slip"* (see Walk 15).

So, continue along the path, looking for these landmarks, the first of which is half a mile away.

At the head of the valley, turn left behind a wooden fence …..

….. and a little further on, after a derelict farmhouse on the left, take another left turn.

We're now on the homeward stretch.

After 300 yards, notice the derelict farm on the slope of the hill to your left. This is Burnt Hill Farm, mentioned by Marshall.

After a short uphill section, where the path bends to the right, ignore the West Pennine Way footpath to the right and continue along the main path.

A little further on, a wall comes into view and, when you reach it, go straight on, so that it is on your right. Walk parallel to the wall for almost half a mile. Twenty yards after it ends, where the path divides, take the left fork down the hill. Soon a wire fence starts on your left and then a wall. Continue with the wall on your left to a gate with a wall-stile to its right. Head down the field, towards a farmhouse, keeping the trees and gulley on your right. At the bottom of the field, bear left through the gate or over the stile into the next small field.

Pass to the right of the farmhouse through a series of gates and continue, keeping a wall on your left. At the kissing gate, bear left down the walled track. At the bottom, emerge onto a short road, bear right onto Park Road then left onto Holcombe Road and return to your starting point.

Folly Clough

Marshall says: *"Our valley possesses an almost unknown wealth of cloughs: on every side the great hills are torn with fissures deep and gloomy, where streams brawl, and tall trees throw their shadows. There is always freshness beneath the trees that shelter them, and quiet in their secluded haunts.*

They have ever been associated with the superstitious and the supernatural. Fairies were supposed to people them, and the boggart was said to make them its home. Little children used to stand peering in terror at their openings, dreading to cross the shadows of the trees that darkened them, and even men of iron nerve cared not to be overtaken in their fastnesses by nightfall. In former days almost every clough had a fairy and a boggart of its own; in many instances the clough deriving its name from the haunting sprite.

I have long held that the strong taste for reading, and for the study of poetry, and botany and geology, for which the Lancashire operative is famous, as well as the passion for rambling, which seems to be so prevalent, are mainly due to these wild stretches and lonely haunts within such easy reach of thousands.

Crawshaw Booth is the best destination for Folly Clough. Arriving there, let the rambler mount the brow as far as the National Schools, and then follow the turn to the right known as Goodshaw Lane. A walk of three hundred yards will bring him to an iron gate leading towards the Folly Mill. Through this gate he must pass, when after skirting the now silent structure, he will find himself looking down into the entrance of the clough. Here the defile is deep and the sides precipitate; the view however is built in, and the beauty destroyed by a wall rising to a height of one hundred feet. This wall unites the banks on either side and was built as a means of transit; but why after this hideous pattern it is hard to say, when a rustic bridge would not only have served the same purpose, but cost at least a third less. At any rate, this blundering and hideous piece of engineering has cost us one of the most beautiful bits of scenery in the valley.

A little higher up, and before reaching Hawthorn Mill, the clough divides, a portion branching off towards what was once known as the Old Hall. In 1856 the Mill was the scene of a terrific boiler explosion, six lives being lost. The old boiler-house still stands in its ruins and may be seen by all who pass through the yard to the clough beyond.

The heart of the clough is now entered, and no other obstruction mars the view, until the rambler reaches the reservoir bank at its head.

The stream is crossed and bay after bay, and vista after vista start into ever-changing view. Two objects of beauty await the observant eye. To the right, a volume of water leaps down a cleft, all rock-walled and tree-girt, while to the right, almost unobservable in overhanging herbage, is hidden the Gin Spa Well. I have often wondered why the name gin is so common to many of the wells in our district. The oldest inhabitants assure me it is not because of the illicit distilleries once so common but because of the clearness of these waters. This Gin Spa Well, however, was supposed to be the well of the fairy of this clough, the famous Jenny Greenteeth who was wont to haunt these shadowy recesses, stealing silently, sometimes invisibly, up their steep sides, to pinch the sleeping children or turn sour the milk in the dairies. The gentleman accompanying me on this ramble, a native of Crawshaw Booth, pointed out places where, as a child, he had in fancy heard the note of approach and looking round, seen the mystic sprite, and where he had fled in precipitate terror from the charm of the Fairy of Folly Clough.

The last stretch of the water careering down this clough is arrow-like in its flow and comes with swift volume from the escape in the reservoir under the bank of which the rambler now stands. From this stream we climbed the bank, and, gaining its summit, came upon one of the finest sweeps of farmland and moorland in the valley.

As we looked across the wide landscape, no form was in view. The scene seemed devoid of human life. There were a few stunted trees, the mapping out of fields by rude stone walling, winding paths and farmsteads, some empty and in ruins. How eloquent are these wastes and wilds, and yet there are thousands in our busy valley who have never climbed to their heights, and who know nothing of their loneliness. In these days of rush and roar, it is needful a man should occasionally frequent them, or he will never know what it is to be alone.

Returning by the old Goodshaw Road, we talked together of the far past. My companion told me that he lived in the house in which he was born, and in which his father and grandfather had been born before him. He had grown up in the district, knowing all its legends and traditions and I was confirmed in a long-cherished idea that true life is indigenous. Immobility may not perhaps people a world with new life and open out the Eldorados of distant shores, but it gives growth to the highest instincts in men and develops a domesticity without which life is shorn of its highest attributes. That it may not lead to breadth of mind is perhaps true; that it cultivates strength of character few will deny; and hence it is we have yet the sturdy yeomen to whom we shall have again to turn for re-peopling the now waste places of our land."

Can we follow his route? Yes. Marshall refers to a reservoir at the top of the clough. This no longer exists but, other than that, I suspect that little has changed in the last one hundred and thirty years.

Walk 17: Circular walk to Folly Clough and Swinshaw Moor

Distance: 3 miles

Features: A haunting and haunted clough and sweeping views on the moor.

Terrain: some fairly steep gradients; stiles and gates; can be very muddy and boggy, sometimes the stream in the Clough is impassable.

Starting point: Crawshawbooth Jubilee Garden. Near-ish postcode BB4 8NE

Parking / Public transport: Park on-street nearby. Crawshawbooth has a regular bus service.

Route: From the bus shelter next to the Golden Jubilee Garden, walk up Burnley Road towards Burnley and, after 300 yards, turn right into Goodshaw Lane. Pass Albert Road on your left and, in another 200 yards, just before the children's play area on your left, where a large hedge on your right ends, turn right onto a wide track.

Immediately before the bridge over the clough, turn left onto a footpath, so that the clough is on your right.

Look back to see the 'wall' that Marshall describes as "*a hideous piece of engineering*", and it's on the front cover of this book.

Follow the path by the side of the clough and then left uphill with a wall on your left. At the top, turn right onto a lane and, in 50 yards, bear right (through the gate / barrier or around it on a short stone path) onto a wide grass track. You soon pass over old concrete foundations which are the remains of Hawthorn Mill.

Continue on the footpath, up the clough, with the stream to your right. After a quarter of a mile, cross the stream via a concrete bridge.

The path on the far bank has been eroded, so you'll need to decide how to re-join it, 20 yards up-stream from the bridge. I had to cross the stream twice after the bridge and then climb the bank. Stones are carefully placed to make this easier and, strangely, they seem to move quite often. I suspect that Jenny Greenteeth, the Fairy of Folly Clough, is still active but is now helping walkers instead of frightening children.

Continue to climb the clough with the stream now on your left. Ascend at the side of the

'staircase' wall and follow a wire fence that is on your right, around to the right until you reach a wider path with a gate to the right. Turn left onto the wide track.

It is wide, straight and relatively flat because it's an old tramway, used for transporting coal from a mine on the moors above, to Crawshawbooth below. Stay on this track for a third of a mile.

Shortly after passing a deep gulley on your right and just before a stone-faced spring in front of you, bear left in a 10 o'clock direction and stay on the broad path towards a small group of trees.

At the trees and a gate / stile, bear left and continue on the wide track (Gib Hill Lane, not signed).

Stay on Gib Hill Lane for over half a mile until it becomes a well-surfaced road with a fenced reservoir building on your right and a farm on your left. Descend to the houses in front of you and turn left onto Goodshaw Lane.

After 200 yards, notice Goodshaw Chapel on your left. It was built in 1760 and is in the care of English Heritage. It's a rare example of an early non-conformist chapel and well worth a visit, which has to be arranged in advance. The grassed area beyond it, was Goodshaw Chapel hamlet referred to in the next chapter. This photograph was taken in the 1890s.

Continue down Goodshaw Lane for half a mile and, where it meets Burnley Road, turn left to return to your starting point.

Goodshaw Fold

Marshall says: *"At the north-east end of our valley, towards the moors of Swinshaw and Hameldon, lie the hamlets of Goodshaw, the one crowning the Morrell Heights, the other almost hidden under the shadow of Love Clough. Both date from a far past, and both have played important parts in the history of Rossendale. In neither, however, does modern life seem to find a congenial home, for civilisation, on the one hand, has descended from Goodshaw Chapel, and on the other ascended from Goodshaw Fold, towards the thriving village of Crawshaw Booth, which lies midway between the hamlets, and on the main road between Manchester and Burnley.*

Not that the Goodshaws are silent and waste: they still possess a life but it is an old-world life. Hence, if anything of their past is to be preserved, it is time the local historian was at work, for each year's recession carries with it stories and histories never more to be recalled.

The pleasantest route to Goodshaw Fold is to alight at the tram terminus and turn down Co-operation Street, rounding the angle of the Friends' Meeting House, and following the bank of the Limy past the Britannia, Alexandra and Stone Holme Mills. Cheerless and uninviting is the initial stage of the journey for these mills are bare of all architectural proportion; and the cottages, barrack like, devoid of all the adornments of home.

Spoliation is the sin of modern manufacture. That men should live none will deny; but that men should live at the expense of life is a travesty of every law of nature and of right. I must own that I never look upon these old mills, and some modern ones, too, without giving vent to a righteous curse. Here I see everything carried out to facilitate money-making and nothing done to insure the comfort of the men and women, and the boys and girls, who are the human factors in its product. Mills are built for machinery and for production and not for those who work therein and thereat.

Nor were the old homes in advance of the old mills. Built back to back, with one room above and one below, in them children were littered and brought up, more by luck than by management. And yet comfort and beauty are not altogether dependent upon expense, but come within the reach of all, and pay good interest on the little invested on their behalf.

Once through the network of mills, the meadows stretch out before the rambler's eye. The path winds beside the river, now black with pollution, such pollution, however, being powerless to destroy its song. It murmurs along in its blackness, singing even in its turbid flow. Nature dies hard. The hand of man has turned this once silvery stream to stenchful slime, but not to silence. Here and there stray trees dot the landscape but in most instances these, too, have yielded to the blast of death, their upper branches smitten, their foliage withering as mown grass.

It seems that nature and commerce are incompatible, for where the latter is established the former dies. This will not always be so. Science is teaching us how to get life out of death, and wealth out of waste. The very products of modern manufacture which we now cast off, and with which we blight our meadows and befoul our rivers, will, before long, be utilised. Gold is hidden in their dross and the refuse that now devours will be changed into those elements of life that renew the face of the earth.

Midway between Stone-Holme and Goodshaw Fold stands a clump of trees. They are the remains of what was once a forest. Here, in summer hours, the children sport and lovers whisper. Through this plantation, we cross the stream by a footbridge and arrive at Gin Clough, so called from the fact that a gin once stood at its foot, worked by its waters. To reach Goodshaw Fold, however, we must again cross the river by Hargreaves Mill, when we are almost within sight of the village.

Leaving the Sliven Clod Road and turning up Love Clough Road we reach another old hall yet in good preservation, though long since denuded of its historic life. It stands fronting the path which we take, and is gabled and mullioned with many fine examples of the builder's art.

In Goodshaw Fold we cannot find a straight bit of street anywhere, the consequence being that it is impossible, from any point, to see what lies ahead. The roads are labyrinthine as a maze, while the back of one house opens upon the front of another, and where we expect to find an outlet we find a cul de sac. There is a general topsy-turvydom, a confusion of arrangement, as it were, each man seeming to have snatched at his part and erected his building without consulting the rights of his neighbours. At one time it was the home of the wealthy, for here is property that dates back to the settlement of some of our leading families of the past.

There is no public-house in Goodshaw Fold, nor has there ever been. This, however, does not seem to have been warrant for good behaviour, for so rough was the element fifty years ago that it was with fear a master passed his own men in the streets after working-hours were over. I was told by one of the oldest inhabitants that her brother was wont many a time to remain indoors of an evening rather than face the rowdy element in the streets, although many of the men composing it were in his employ.

The whole Fold may be traversed in a few minutes, but those minutes will be sure to rouse rich memories.

Talking with an old inhabitant about this once richly-wooded district, and enquiring the cause of its present denudation, I was told that, many years ago, a firm of cloggers settled in the neighbourhood, bought up the trees, and felled them for "the wooden shoon" of the operative and labouring classes. Here again the beauty of our valley has been sacrificed to utility and worn away in the ceaseless tramp of its inhabitants. We all know men must be shod, whether by means of *tree trunks or cow hides; but is it not strange that it seldom enters into the brain of man to replace his tree with a sapling, as he replaces his cow with a calf?*

Following the windings of the Love Clough Road, the rambler enters the cleft, across which is built the famous printworks, Great Clough lying beyond, and losing itself in Goodshaw Hill. Instead of passing through the printworks yard, the higher footpath must be taken, which skirts a lodge and leads out towards the old Love Clough Hall. On the farther side of the stream, which is here clear as crystal, and standing upon a terraced bank, the building presents an ideal picture and, but for the adjoining printworks, a man might fancy himself in some West of England nook, or even a far-off spot in Wales.

When first I came into Rossendale I was much taken with the name Love Clough. I associated it with romance, and with village Romeos and Juliets. Upon looking up the name, however, the glamour was shed. It was not Love Clough, I found, the clough where lovers lingered and whispered, but Lough Clough, the clough "where the waters lay". So is our idealism shattered in this common-place world."

Can we follow his route? Yes, although we divert around a new housing development. The building thought to be 'Love Clough Hall' is now a social club. Built in 1741 as the 'Mansion House' they are probably one and the same. The river that we follow is 'Limy Water', one Rossendale's three main rivers.

Walk 18: Crawshawbooth to Goodshaw Fold and Loveclough

Distance: 3 miles (there and back)

Features: Victorian mills, a rural riverside path and an 18th century hall.

Terrain: mostly flat; some gates and stiles; can be a bit muddy.

Starting point: Crawshawbooth Jubilee Garden. Near-ish postcode BB4 8NE

Parking / Public transport: Park on-street nearby. Crawshawbooth has a regular bus service.

Route: From the Jubilee Garden (next to the bus shelter) in the centre of Crawshawbooth, walk up Burnley Road towards Burnley and turn left into Co-operation Street. In 80 yards, the Friends Meeting House is on your right. This photograph was taken in the 1890s.

Turn right onto a lane (Stoneholme Road), so that the river is on your left. Walk through an industrial area, then pass a row of terraced cottages, Stone Holme Terrace, on your right. Continue, keeping the river on your left.

In 400 yards, where the wood on the other side of the river ends, and a road bears to the left over a bridge, go straight on, keeping the river on your left. The valley on the other side of the river is Gin Clough.

Stay on the track for a quarter of a mile, passing industrial units, until you reach a short cobbled section and a T junction. Turn left.

This is Goodshaw Fold. As you walk down the lane, notice the water fountain on your right, known locally as 'the spewing duck'. This photograph was also taken in the 1890s.

Just before the two bridges over the stream, turn right onto Love Clough Road (signed on a house on the right). Bear right in front of a bungalow and then diagonally left after it. Our path is to the left of the next house.

Cross the stile and continue on the broad grass track for 300 yards with a meadow on your left. Pass to the right of the houses and continue for a quarter of a mile, keeping a tall fence on your left, eventually emerging onto a road (Commercial Street). Turn left. Within a few yards, the Social Club to your right, on the other side of the stream, is almost certainly Marshall's 'Love Clough Hall'.

We will return by the same route, the main points of which are:

- walk back up Commercial Street and take the footpath on the right, then keep the fence on your right
- at the end of the meadow, cross the stile and at the bungalow on your right, bear left
- turn left onto Goodshaw Fold Road and, after 80 yards, turn right across the cobbled section
- stay on this track for almost a mile, keeping the river on your right, then turn left at the Friends Meeting House and return to your starting point.

Tunstead Tops

Marshall says: *"At the foot of Sow Clough and beneath the shadow of Mitchell-Field Nook, stands an old hall embowered in trees, known as Honey Hole. It is one of the most sequestered spots in Rossendale, and was, when insect life was rife in the valley, a favourite resort of bees. It stands behind the uplands of Waggoner Tunstead, and fronts a wooded glen, down which course waters from the "Top th' Bank," while on either side rise the shoulders of sheltering hills which break the blast and stay the storm.*

On the morning of this my ramble, as I faced the house, I took note of its style and dimensions. No date was discoverable and the only fact of interest I could gather was that even now in hot weather the old honey stains of two hundred years ago reappear upon the surface of the yard flags.

Proceeding through the grounds and plantation, and upwards past the outlying shippon, I reached the ruins of the old Union Workhouse at Mitchell-Field. When compared with the present noble structure at Pike Law by which it has been supplanted, some idea is gained of the great change which a few years has wrought in the care for and condition of the poor.

There is a legendary interest associated with Mitchell-Field Nook. It was the site originally chosen by the inhabitants upon which to build their first church in 1510 and to which they accordingly conveyed their materials for its erection. No sooner, however, was this done, than busy workers in the night hours mysteriously removed the materials to the other side of the valley and placed them in the croft where the present church now stands. Nothing daunted, the determined builders re-conveyed them to Mitchell-Field, appointing one of their number to keep watch and to raise an alarm should any further attempt at removal be made. But the watch slumbered, the genii returned to their labours and successfully defeated, for a second time, the purpose of the enterprising parishioners. With a determination characteristic of the inhabitants of Rossendale, the materials were brought back once more and the watch increased to three, to whom were given the strictest orders that no stone was to be touched, and that all meddlesome folk were to be driven from the ground. Not long had they been at work, when an old woman silently stole in amongst them and wished them a "good evening," offering them food, which was enchanted; and no sooner had they partaken than sleep closed their eyes, and again, for the third time, their purposes were defeated. So the church was built where the spirits decreed, and the old Hebrew truth was again illustrated, "Except the Lord build the house, they labour in vain that build it."

Passing the ruined workhouse and the originally proposed site of the first church of our valley, I reached the "Tops", a little above the watercourse that leaps over and falls into the disused quarry. A wild expanse of moorland now opened before me.

I followed the path to Brex and then made towards the gorge which seams these wastes and opens out towards the Shaw Clough Mill. I had not gone far, however, before I stopped to contemplate the Isles from this altered and nearer point of view. They rise in oval mounds and resemble the breasts of a recumbent giantess slumbering on the expanse of sunny moor. These Isles are well-known and imposing landmarks, and visible for many miles.

Scattered over these tops are many quaint farmsteads, bearing still quainter names. I often muse upon their origin and history, wondering who was engulfed at "Slip-in," and what the culinary ability of the good housewife once living at "Salt Pie Hall" or what fool's history is associated with "Folly Clough."

But I must continue my ramble, and in doing so follow the windings of Bridge Clough. At first the stream is silent, shallow, and sluggish but as the gorge deepened, fan-tailed falls shot over into the lower levels and a wild confusion of strata began to buttress up the glen; while overgrowths of foliage lent added gloom and glory to the scene.

I now passed to the ruined mills and lodges damming up the lower falls. They took me back to the time when the clough resounded with the whirl of many wheels and the ring of many voices; when once, a hive of industry, it yielded livelihood to neighbouring villages and sent out its productions to the markets of the world; when, with increased demand, there was a quickened revolution of its machinery; and, alas, when new inventions, refusing to limit themselves to its size and strength, left it to "cold, continual peace.'

I know the Tunstead Tops possess but little charm to the rambler. They are not easy of reach; and, when reached, they are neither picturesque nor sheltered. But there is freedom on their breezy heights, while from the level of their tableland the spectator stands amid an amphitheatre of hills.

Can we follow his route? Only partially. We pass Honey Hole and Mitchell-Field Nook and visit Marshall's 'Tops' but, after that, despite the fact that the area is criss-crossed by designated footpaths, obstructions and lack of regular use mean that it is very difficult to find, never-mind follow, them. Even if we could walk across the tops to Bridge Clough, we can't wander along it as Marshall did. So, we must be content with a somewhat sanitised and shorter route. Having said that, it is worth the effort, as this is a lovely, secluded part of Rossendale, with far-reaching views, that is rarely visited.

Walk 19: Circular walk from Stacksteads to the Tunstead Tops

Distance: 2.3 miles

Features: Rural lanes, a deep clough and impressive views.

Terrain: Some not-too-steep gradients; gates and stiles; mostly surfaced paths and tracks.

Starting point: The junction of Booth Road and Newchurch Road (A681), Stacksteads. Near-ish postcode OL13 0NA

Parking / Public transport: Park on-street nearby. This road junction is on a bus route.

Route: From the road junction, walk up Booth Road and, immediately after the school on the right (Stacksteads Church of England Primary School), turn right into a short lane which then becomes a footpath. Pass the school playing field on your right and continue straight on when it becomes a grass footpath.

After 200 yards the path emerges into a yard with a house on the left. Turn right, up the concrete drive, through a gate, then turn left in front of a house, Honey Hole Barn. Our next path isn't immediately obvious but is in the top left corner opposite the house.

Walk up the path with a wall to your right and a deep clough to your left until you reach Mitchell-Field Nook cottages on your right. Turn left over a bridge then left again down a track, so that the clough is now on your left. Descend to the first house on your left and turn sharp right, in a 4 o'clock direction, up a farm lane. In 100 yards, turn right in front of a barn and head up the hill on a track.

Keeping a fence and / or wall on your left, continue up the hill.

After almost half a mile, as you approach a farmhouse and the track bends to the right towards it, stay close to the wall on your left and cross a stile in the top left corner, opposite the house. Turn left from your previous direction of travel.

Walk along the track, parallel to the wall on your left and, in 100 yards, bear left onto a wider track. Once over the brow of the hill, descend, keeping a fence on your left and then follow the lane around a sharp left bend, towards a farm.

Pass through the farmyard and walk down the lane for a third of a mile. After it bends gently to the left, you reach a junction where the lane bends sharply down to the right. Don't follow it. Go straight across down the wide tarmac drive to the left of the house in front of you. At the end of a small wall on your left, go through the gap and up the concrete steps to join a footpath.

Cross the footbridge over a stream and up the hill, then bear right onto a road. Pass through farm buildings then bear right down the hill. In 120 yards, at the lane 'T' junction, turn right and descend. Ignore the farm lane to the left and soon join a housing estate road (Tunstead Road, not signed). Turn left and follow the road round to the right. Turn left into Haworth Drive (signed on the side of a house on your left).

After 30 yards, bear left onto a paved footpath with houses on your left. Where the path joins another, bear right and descend to Booth Road. Turn left to return to your starting point.

The Fairy Palaces of Rossendale

Marshall climbs part-way up Cribden, after dark, to watch the gas lights of the cotton mills illuminate the Valley and he muses on the mill-girls, the fairies of the fairy palaces, who work in them. His commentary is philosophical and insightful and his views are surprisingly modern. Marshall's vantage point is Hazel Head, just half a mile from Rawtenstall's town centre. He is struck by the sight and the silence. Today, the sight is worth the climb, day or night, but distant traffic noise means that we can only occasionally experience his silence.

Marshall says: *"I retain a vivid recollection of two railway journeys made some years ago at night-fall through three of the busiest and wealthiest counties of our land. The first whirled me by the pit-fires and smelting furnaces of Durham and Northumberland, and the second conveyed me from Bolton to Todmorden, through a well-nigh unbroken succession of the gas-illuminated cotton factories of Lancashire. At the time I made these journeys I was a stranger to the sights and surroundings through which I passed; yet, despite my location since, both amid collieries and manufactories, the phenomena I then for the first time witnessed, the vivid flames of the one and the fiery-like apparition of the other, left an impression upon my mind I have never lost. Nor has my acquaintance with factories led to my detestation of them, though I am willing to confess that if I were* *compelled to be in them oftener, I should be prone to like them less.*

Yet, after all, there is a poetry about them, as about all things else. Granted that in the day-time they look repulsive in their drear and grimy garb, gaunt and square and many storied; yet with night-fall their hideousness is hidden, while their long rows of windows, ablaze with light, remind one of the illuminated palaces of fabled fairy-land.

To stand upon some point of vantage and look down into the valleys as they rapidly fill with mist, accustoming the sight to the darkness, the valley lies mapped out before the eye, but the lines in which it is drawn are no longer sharp and definite, they are lines of fire. If the reader does not credit my statement or thinks me too enthusiastic in my description of this wondrous sight, let him accompany me round Hazel Head.

It is an afternoon late in January. The sun has already gone down, but the after-glow remains, and tints the landscape before us with varying shades, colouring the scattered lodges and reservoirs that lie in the nooks and hollows, and here and there playing upon the window-panes of cottages, high-seated upon the tops, until they burn with the radiance of a beacon flame. Let us linger for a moment over the familiar land-marks ere they vanish.

Yonder is the Chapel Hill, where after life's fitful fever many a noble soul sleeps well. Above, and a little to the right, lies Seat Naze, with its crowning tuft of stunted trees, the tower of Newchurch sheltering below. On the opposite range rises the oval form of Cowpe, that mountain of the moorlands, the hills beneath sloping off towards Windy Harbour, then falling at the foot of Edenfield and Ewood Bridge.

The scattered mansions of the rich look cold and lonesome in their scantily-wooded demesnes, and the irregular lines of cottages, wherein dwell the artisans, die away as they precipitately dip in slanting rows into the valley beneath. But the air is chill, and as we have a few moments to wait for the sight for which we are on the look-out, we secure another button on our coats. As we look out upon the darkness, spell-bound by the silence, a firmament of light breaks out below us, and it seems as though the earth had its stars as well as the heavens. Momentarily, with unseen hands, a long line of flame flashes out upon the night. A moment more, and a second, a third, a fourth line starts into view, parallel and equidistant, together building up a four-square block, illumined and bold. Ere we grow accustomed to the sight, another, and another, and yet another block of flame breaks in upon our startled gaze, until the mills of Ilex, Hall Carr, Rawtenstall, and Newchurch Company's, form a continuous, nay, an almost unbroken, wall of light.

0, what a sight is this, a sight to stir a poet's heart; a sight of which every inhabitant of Rossendale may well be proud, and one which he cannot too often seize a chance to view. "The fairy palaces of Rossendale" I said to myself.

A few years ago, I stood in an excited crowd witnessing an old mill as it was rapidly consumed by the flames. A number of elderly women were near me, and I was soon attracted towards them by their sobs and lamentations. On inquiring the cause of their trouble, I found that, when girls, they had worked in the mill that was now perishing amid the tongues of fire, and that, next to their own homes, their fondest memories and happiest associations were wrapped up in it. There, prosaic reader, you have an instance of the poetry of factory life.

But I cannot stay my pen in its description of the fairy palaces of Rossendale without a word or two about the fairies themselves. If there is no poetry associated with the palaces, there is a great deal of poetry associating itself with those whose fingers ply the looms and tend the busy wheels. I admit that poets have never been enamoured of shawls and clogs, nor are these articles of apparel, according to the lore of elf-land, the dress of fays and fairies. But the poetry of life lies deeper than this, it is the poetry of the heart; and to me there are few sights and sounds more stirring than those accompanying the 'losing' of the mills, when hundreds of hurrying feet clatter along the pavement, and hundreds of merry voices ring out into the air, and the fairies are free.

True, they may jostle against you in their hurry, and should you chance to be a man of eccentric habit and *dress, as I am, your eccentricities may call forth criticisms more just than pleasant. But if there is a vein of mirth in your nature, or a sympathetic spasm in your heart for the rising race, you will stand the jostling good humoured]y, and take the jokes as to your appearance with a laugh, and offer a prayer for the toiling youth of our busy valley.*

But if I wanted to introduce a stranger to the fairies of Rossendale, I should introduce him to them on a Sunday afternoon, when the schools are filled with their pleasant faces and resound with their cheerful songs, "These, sir," I should say to him, "are the girls of Lancashire; match them if you can in any other county in the realm." And I am sure if he had travelled up and down the land as much as I have, he would find his sentiments echoed in the refrain of the old song, which I heard sung when a child, about "The Lancashire lass, which none can surpass."

None know Lancashire aright who know her not in her Sunday garb. I love her in her week-day garb of grime and gloom, her dirt and din are dear to me; but I love her most in the quiet of her Sabbaths, when the air is clear, the chimneys smokeless, and the ponderous engines rest; when her toiling thousands, freed from labour, roam her fields and fells, and her sons and daughters, in scattered groups, wend their way to Sabbath school, and the day of rest spreads abroad its hallowed, calm delight."

Can we follow his route? Marshall doesn't tell us which path he took from his home in Rawtenstall to

Hazel Head. Today, there is an easy-to-follow (even in the dark) route which we will use. There are no lights once we leave the streets, so you'll need a torch.

Walk 20: Rawtenstall Market to Hazel Head

Distance: 1 mile (there and back)

Features: an impressive view of Rawtenstall and far beyond.

Terrain: some steep gradients; some uneven ground; sometimes a bit muddy.

Starting point: Rawtenstall Market, Newchurch Road, Rawtenstall. Near-ish postcode BB4 7QX.

Parking / Public transport: park nearby in a public car park (during the day-time, you'll need a parking disc obtainable from local shops) or on-street nearby. Rawtenstall Bus Station and the East Lancs Railway Station are less than half a mile away.

Route: From the traffic lights near the Market, walk up Haslingden Old Road and turn sharp right (almost back on yourself) at the first road on the right, Whittle Street. At the top of the street, turn right onto Greenfield Street, then immediately left onto Beech Street. After 120 yards, where Prospect Road joins from the right, bear left in a 10 o'clock direction, pass

the garages on your right and join a track which meanders and climbs up the hill.

Pass the communications mast on your right. The path bends to the left then straightens out and, in 50 yards, at the top of a steep section, there are gates to your left and right. We have reached our destination.

In Marshall's day, this was the location of two farms, Higher Hazel Head and Lower Hazel Head. Enjoy the view, day or night. Return to your starting point by the same route.

About me

I have walked Rossendale's hills for thirty years and my only qualification for writing this book is the knowledge I've gained whilst doing so.

I've written almost one hundred photo-history booklets about various UK towns and cities. These can be purchased on the internet via my website. Titles include: Jersey in 1921; The Way We Were: Manchester; Victorian Walks on the Isle of Wight; The River Thames from Source to Sea; How they built the Forth Railway Bridge; Victorian Whitby through the Magic Lantern …. and many, many more.

I'm a Victorian 'magic lantern' showman, a lecturer on pre-cinema entertainments and I run our family business 'The Keasbury-Gordon Photograph Archive'.

You can contact me via my website 'Magic Lantern World' at www.magiclanternist.com

Marshall Mather left a wonderful legacy in his books and it has been a privilege to retrace his steps. I have discovered footpaths, hidden nooks and industrial archaeology that I was previously unaware of and shared his delight in, and awe of, Rossendale's tranquil valleys and spectacular hill-top vistas.

I agree with him when he says *"The inhabitants, if they only knew it, are among the highly-favoured of the earth."*

Have fun out there and stay safe.

Printed in Poland
by Amazon Fulfillment
Poland Sp. z o.o., Wrocław